Centipedes

The summer is hot, but the creek is cool and shady. You sit quietly, watching different kinds of animals. A two-legged bird sits on a tree branch. A four-legged squirrel climbs a tree. An eight-legged spider spins a beautiful web in the branches. You turn over a rock, and a small creature scurries away. It doesn't have two legs or even eight—it has dozens! What kind of strange creature is this? It's a centipede!

What Are Centipedes?

Centipedes look like insects, but they are not. Instead, many scientists think centipedes are more closely related to lobsters and shrimp. Insects such as ants and house flies have three body areas and six legs. Centipedes, however, have just two body areas—the head and the body itself. A centipede's body is made up of sections called **segments**. Each segment looks like a little ring.

Each segment also has its own legs! The segment has two legs—one on each side. With its many segments, a centipede can have over 40 legs. Some different types, or **species**, of centipedes have close to 100 legs! In fact, the name "centipede" means "hundred feet." Different centipede species have different numbers of legs.

This ground centipede is looking for something to eat. ⇒

A centipede's head has long feelers, or **antennae**. Behind the head are poisonous claws. A centipede's body is also covered with a hard, protective shell called an **exoskeleton**. Centipedes' bodies are usually gray or reddish brown, and are often about an inch long. One kind of centipede—the *giant centipede* of South America—can grow to over 10 inches long!

⇐ Here you can see the underside of a giant desert centipede. You can clearly see its poisonous claws, which have black, pointed tips.

What Do Centipedes Eat?

Centipedes are **predators** that hunt and kill other insects. They must move fast to catch their dinner. Larger centipedes even hunt frogs, mice, lizards, and snakes! The centipede's flat body lets it squeeze into cracks and holes looking for food. Once the centipede finds an insect it can eat, it grabs it in its powerful claws. Then it shoots poison into the insect to kill it.

This house centipede has caught a bug for its meal. ⇒

Where Do Centipedes Live?

Centipedes live in most areas where the weather is warm or hot. They are common in Central and South America, Africa, Europe, and the United States. Centipedes need moisture to live. If they are trapped in a dry house, they often shrivel up and die. Usually they hide outside in damp areas or in rotting dead plant material. Good places to find centipedes are under rocks, in rotting logs, in leaf piles, or in damp, dark basements.

This large centipede lives in Malaysia. ⇒

A few centipede species give birth to live babies. Most, however, lay eggs in dirt or rotting wood. Female centipedes lay about 40 eggs at a time. After she lays all of her eggs, the mother curls up around them to protect them. From time to time she licks the eggs to keep them clean. Finally, after several weeks or months, the eggs hatch.

What Are Baby Centipedes Like?

In many centipede species, the mother stays around and cares for her babies once they hatch. The babies look like adults, except that they have only a few body segments and a couple of legs. Soon, however, the young begin to **molt**, or shed their outgrown skins to reveal newer, larger skins. Each time they molt, they get more body segments and legs. The babies molt seven to ten times before they become adults. Adult centipedes can live for over six years.

Top: These young centipedes live in South Africa. ⇒

Bottom: Here you can see a giant centipede that has shed its skin.

Are Centipedes Different From Millipedes?

Centipedes and millipedes are very different animals. Centipedes are skinny and flat. Millipedes have longer, rounder bodies. Each segment in a millipede's body has four legs instead of two. A millipede's exoskeleton is much harder than a centipede's. Millipedes' legs and antennae are shorter than those of centipedes. Also, millipedes do not have poisonous claws.

⇐ This giant millipede lives in Brazil.

Even though they have more legs, millipedes move more slowly than centipedes. Since millipedes are such slow movers, they often cannot escape from their enemies by running away. Instead, millipedes protect themselves in other ways. Often they curl into a tight ball. Then their hard, protective shell is the only thing a predator can reach.

Millipedes also have openings on the sides of their bodies that let out bad-smelling, bad-tasting liquids. These liquids quickly change an enemy's mind about eating such a bad-tasting animal!

This millipede is protecting itself. It has rolled into a tight ball. ⇒

Unlike centipedes, millipedes are **scavengers**. They eat mostly dead, **decaying** plants and insects. Millipedes often dig through leaf and garbage piles looking for food. Sometimes millipedes damage or even kill young plants by eating the new roots or leaves.

Do Centipedes Have Enemies?

Many animals such as frogs, birds, lizards, and small rodents eat centipedes. Because so many animals eat them, centipedes have developed ways of protecting themselves. If they can, centipedes squeeze their flat bodies into tiny spaces to hide from enemies. They use their speed to run away. If they are trapped, they attack with their poisonous claws. Their poison is not deadly to humans, but it can kill many smaller creatures. Some centipede species break off their own legs! The legs wiggle and distract the enemy while the centipede escapes.

⇐ This giant desert centipede is scurrying to hide under a rock.

Are Centipedes Dangerous?

Some people keep large centipede species as pets. Most people, however, consider them to be household pests. Centipedes often hide in corners or in laundry baskets, boxes, or shoes. They actually eat many harmful household insects, but people don't like being startled or perhaps bitten by them.

House centipedes like this one might live in your home. ⇒

Like most animals, centipedes don't really belong in houses. Instead, they belong outside, where they can eat dangerous or bothersome insects. No matter how weird or scary they might look, centipedes are an interesting and important part of the natural world.

⇐ Here you can see the head and legs of a centipede as it crawls on a branch in Peru.

Glossary

antennae (an-TEN-nee)
Antennae are long feelers used to sense other objects. Centipedes have antennae on their heads.

decaying (dee-KAY-ing)
When something is decaying, it is rotting. Many millipedes eat decaying plants.

exoskeleton (eks-oh-SKEL-eh-tun)
An exoskeleton is a hard outer covering some animals have instead of bones. Centipedes and millipedes have exoskeletons.

molt (MOLT)
When an animal molts, it sheds its outer layer of skin, fur, or feathers. Young centipedes molt several times as they grow into adults.

predators (PRED-uh-terz)
Predators are animals that hunt and kill other animals. Centipedes are predators.

scavengers (SKAV-en-jerz)
Scavengers are animals that eat trash or decaying plants and animals. Millipedes are scavengers.

segments (SEG-ments)
Segments are separate parts that make up something larger. A centipede's body has many segments.

species (SPEE-sheez)
A species is a different kind of an animal. There are many different species of centipedes.

Index

Web Sites

Visit our homepage for lots of links about centipedes!

http://www.childsworld.com/links.html

Note to Parents, Teachers, and Librarians:
We routinely verify our Web links to make sure they're safe, active sites—
so encourage your readers to check them out!